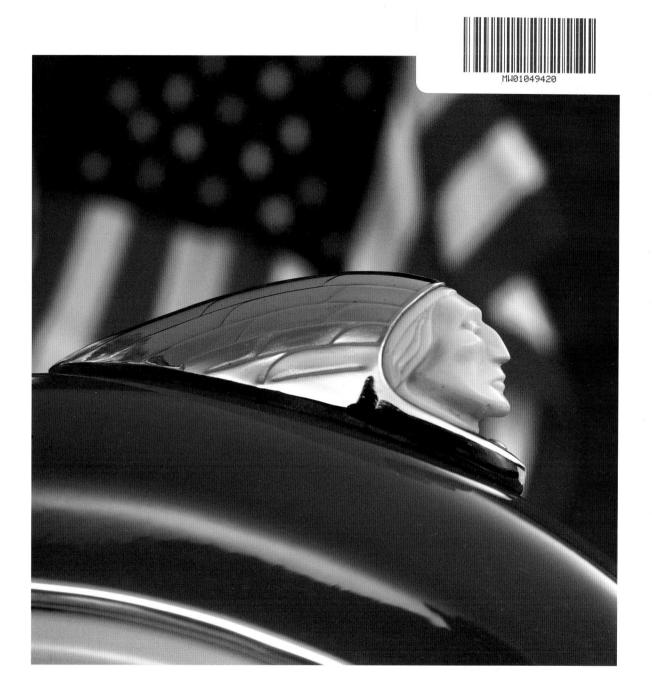

INDIAN
MOTORCYCLES

Buzz Kanter

Motorbooks International
Publishers & Wholesalers ®

First published in 1993 by Motorbooks International
Publishers & Wholesalers, PO Box 2,
729 Prospect Avenue, Osceola, WI 54020 USA

Motorbooks International books are also available
at discounts in bulk quantity for industrial or sales-
promotional use. For details write to Special Sales
Manager at the Publisher's address

Printed and bound in Hong Kong

Library of Congress Cataloging-in-Publication Data

Kanter, Buzz.
    Indian motorcycles / Buzz Kanter.
       p.   cm. — (Enthusiast color series)
    Includes index.
    ISBN 0-87938-827-7
    1. Indian motorcycle—History. I. Title. II. Series.
TL448.I5K36   1993
629.227'5—dc20   93-13071

On the front cover: Gary Stark's 1947 Chief,
superbly painted in a blue and yellow Rainbow paint
scheme by Gary's father, Bob. *Roy Kidney*

On the frontispiece: The Indian head fenderpiece
here may look original, but it's not. It's a one-piece
reproduction offered by Starklite Cycles. The
difference between this and the original (very hard
to find) piece is that the stock Indian part came in two
halves that were glued together at the factory. With
time, the glue turned a darker color, leaving a streak
in the center. *Roy Kidney*

On the title page: A 1936 Indian Chief rebuilt from
a basket case by owner Elmer Lower of Etters,
Pennsylvania. *Jeff Hackett*

On the back cover: A beautiful 1936 Chief restored
by owner Elmer Lower of Etters, Pennsylvania.
Jeff Hackett

Contents

Introduction

While it has been some four decades since the last new Iron Redskin thundered out of the Springfield, Massachusetts, factory, the Indian lore has never died out.

If you have ever ridden a shiny red Chief or nimble Scout, no explanation is needed—you have experienced something that remains a dream for many motorcycle enthusiasts.

If you are one of the thousands that are still looking forward to your first Indian ride, read on and let your imagination carry you along with this remarkable marque.

I think my friend Joshua Placa captured the Indian spirit best when he wrote in the first issue of *Indian Motorcycle Illustrated*: "Indian was much more than a brand—it captured an era, a time when a man could climb aboard his big red Chief, with its streamlined, stylized fenders, kick over the Flathead and feel more free and alive than he'd ever felt before. . . . There was, and still is, an essence about Indian that came right out of the heart of Americana. A mighty spirit dwelled in the Indian soul, and it gave its riders a passionate sense of being on something more than a machine."

I would like to acknowledge and thank the folks that helped put this book together: Mort Wood of the Antique Motorcycle Club for the early years chapter; Robin Markey of Bob's Indian in Etters, Pennsylvania, for the Scout chapter; Randy Zorn of Indian Motorcycle Restoration Company for the Chief chapter; Rudy Litke for the Indian Four chapter; Rick Hvolbeck, Elmer Lower, and Greg Mazza for their advice; the following talented photographers—Jeff Hackett, David Ruzga, Roy Kidney, and Gary Phelps; Motorbooks editor Greg Field, who put it together; and Mark Marselli from *American Iron Magazine*, who helped out on the editing.

Opposite page
The speedometer on a former-police 1937 Sport Four. *Jeff Hacket*

Chapter 1

The Early Years of Indian Motorcycles

The Hendee Manufacturing Company began producing the Indian Motocycle (note no *r*) at the dawn of the new century. The name Indian was chosen to typify its American origin. George M. Hendee, a prominent bicycle manufacturer from Springfield, Massachusetts, and Oscar Hedstrom, a precision toolmaker from Middletown, Connecticut, met in December 1900. Hedstrom had constructed an unusually reliable motor-driven pacer for bicycle races that had greatly impressed Hendee. An agreement was made to produce a simple, practical motorcycle for the average person.

The first machine was completed in the spring of 1901. Following rigorous tests and numerous demonstrations, George Hendee predicted a great future for the new industry, and how right he was!

The first production year was 1902, during which the company built 143 machines. These first Indian motorcycles were powered by 13-cubic-inch engines that boasted 1.75 horsepower. For the first several years, the engines and carburetors were manufactured for Indian by the Aurora Automatic Machinery Company of Aurora, Illinois because Hendee's Springfield factory did not yet have the facilities to produce their own engines.

Motorcycle production more than doubled to 377 in 1903, followed by another significant increase to 546 in 1904.

Opposite page
This jump-start, direct-drive bike is a "straight single," as opposed to some of the twin-engine Indians that were adapted into singles. Back then, if a racer wanted to get a bike into a class like the 350–500cc, the wrench would pull the front cylinder off and cover the hole with a plate. The flywheel then had to be rebalanced to make up for the missing weight. The low-compression engine was relatively easy to start and was said to be very forgiving. *Jeff Hackett*

1905 was an important year for Indian. This was the year they introduced the left-hand twist-grip throttle and cartridge forks, marking the first motorcycle with suspension of any type. By that time, the Indian factory was getting more involved in competition, and, as the saying goes, "competition builds better bikes." Their victories paid off on the sales floor. There was such a demand for these successful Indians that impatient enthusiasts resorted to being added to waiting lists.

For 1906 the engine size was increased to 19 cubic inches, with a subsequent increase to 2.25-horsepower output. The first twin-cylinder model was introduced with a 30-cubic-inch displacement and 3.5-horsepower output. Due to their strong demand for Indian motorcycles, the Hendee Manufacturing Company built a large new factory on State Street in Springfield in 1907. The new factory's size and machinery enabled Hendee to sever his ties with the Aurora Company and manufacture his own engines.

The following year, with the factory finished and tooling set up for new engine manufacturing, all the Indians were built under one roof for the first time.

In 1908 Indian offered a newly designed 3.5-horsepower, single-cylinder machine that proved to be very popular. Orders were so strong that the new plant was forced to run extra shifts through the night to keep up with demand. Indian victories in all forms of competition continued to boost Indian's sales.

The 1909 sales catalog asked the question, "How fast can the Indian run?" The factory's printed answer was simply, "This depends on the skill and courage of the rider! The small single is capable of 45 miles per hour, while the largest machines can probably go much faster than anyone would dare drive them!" This was the same year Indian made a major step in the evolution from motor-powered bicycle to motorcycle by offering an all new loop frame as well as the old bicycle diamond frame. It was the last year the diamond frame was offered by Indian.

There were several improvements made to Indian's frame in 1910. They included the Indian cradle-spring fork and their two-speed gearbox with free engine clutch. These machines were so popular that the following year Indian boasted that over sixty police departments were using Indian motorcycles.

Improvements and refinements continued during the next two years and sales continued to soar. In 1913, Indian introduced the rear-cradle-spring frame and had become the largest manufacturer of motorcycles in the world, producing over 35,000 machines. That figure represented 42 percent of the total domestic production and was an all-time high for Indian. That year there were still over forty other makes being manufactured in the United States.

The Hendee Special was introduced in 1914. It was a 7-horsepower twin-cylinder with battery-powered lights and electrics,

This 1914 Single was a board-track racer. While its civilian counterpart was capable of speeds of maybe 50 miles per hour, this racer was able to go as fast as 80. Back then, neither racer nor stocker was capable of hitting high rpm, but the alcohol-burning race single produced lots of torque. It took a brave person to race this machine, with its total-loss oil system. Many accidents, including fatalities, contributed to the sport's demise. *Jeff Hackett*

> B uilt for a public accustomed to the bicycle and unfamiliar with the mysteries of the internal combustion engine, the early Indians were right on target. These motorcycles were friendly in appearance, and the precision of construction was obvious.
>
> —Jerry Hatfield,
> *Illustrated Indian Motorcycle Buyer's Guide*

and it boasted an electric start. Unfortunately, the battery technology was still too undeveloped. The batteries could not supply the required amount of current to consistently start the machine, so the factory was forced to replace the electrical starters with a kick starter.

Sales began to noticeably decrease, reflecting competition from inexpensive automobiles. This sales decline would continue into the 1920s.

From 1901 until 1915 Indian's motorcycles had progressed from a basic light motor-powered bicycle to a 61-cubic-inch, three-speed, twin-cylinder machine capable of 60 miles per hour. The original Hedstrom pocket-valve engine had been developed and refined to the limit, and the company knew it was time for a significant change.

Indian introduced their highly advanced Powerplus engine in 1916. It was a handsome and powerful flathead, side-valve engine. Unlike its predecessors it sported a clean and uncluttered look, without external moving parts. This was the machine on which the legendary Erwin G. "Cannon Ball" Baker established many coast-to-coast and cross-country records.

The United States entered World War I in 1917, and Indian supplied the US Army with 41,000 motorcycles, more than all the other motorcycle manufacturers combined. By the end of the Great War, Charles B. Franklin, Indian's new chief engineer, began designing and developing his soon-to-be-famous Scout.

Nineteen twenty-two saw the advent of the new 61-cubic-inch Chief. The Powerplus, which had come to be known as the "Old War Horse," was renamed the Standard and positioned as a machine for commercial purposes. It continued in Indian's line until 1924.

By the end of the second decade, with the Great War over and new models on Springfield's drawing boards, there was a feeling of great prosperity and optimism at Indian.

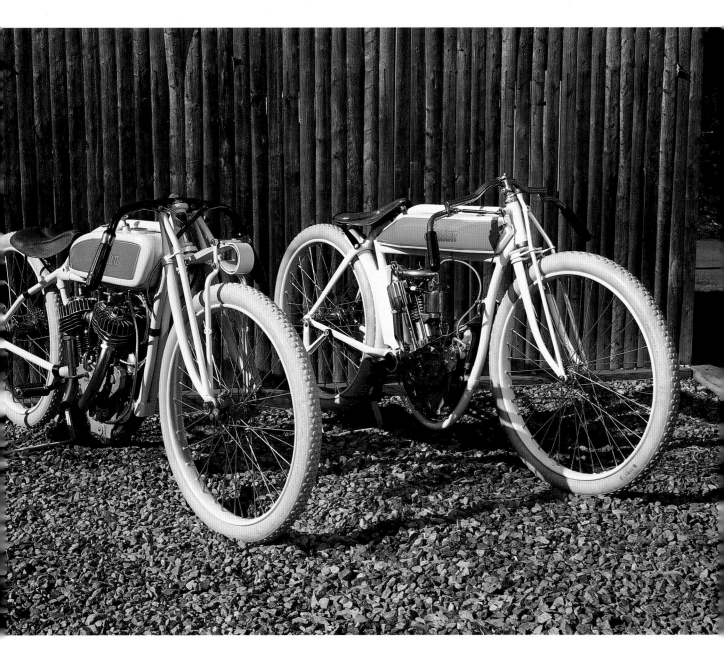

The racing engines were geared so that even at an idle they could speed along at 30 miles per hour. That was accomplished through changes to the timing and cams. Next to this 1914 Single is a 1924 Twin, part of the Steve McQueen collection, which features a Daytona racing frame and special heads. *Jeff Hackett*

Chapter 2

Indian Racing Motorcycles

The founders of the Indian Motocycle Company—George Hendee and Oscar Hedstrom—met at a bicycle race, and Indian motorcycles soon became closely associated with virtually all forms of motorcycle racing.

Records started falling immediately. The year after Indian was started, three of their 1902 single-cylinder, 15.85-cubic-inch-displacement, 1.75-horsepower machines were entered in the first public motorcycle race. It started in New York City and ended in Boston. All three Indian machines finished the contest with perfect scores.

The following year George Holden rode an Indian to set the first long-distance track record, having ridden 150 miles and 75 yards in four hours.

In 1904 an Indian-mounted rider set the one-mile speed record with a blistering time of a shade over one minute and nine seconds.

By 1906 Louis J. Mueller of Cleveland, Ohio, and George Holden of Springfield, Massachusetts, held the record from New York to San Francisco with their new two-cylinder Indians. They covered the 3,476 miles in thirty-one days, twelve hours, and fifteen minutes. The record held for several years.

By 1908 Indian shook off any pretensions that racing wasn't important to them. That year they offered full-out racers for sale to the general public as either a 30.5-cubic-inch single-cylinder or an all-new 61-cubic-inch twin.

Opposite page
This striking 1908 diamond-framed factory racer, which was restored by Stephen Wright, is likely the rarest Indian motorcycle racer in existence. It was built to compete on the board tracks, and is markedly different from the civilian model offered the same year. This Indian was made towards the end of the era when motorcycles were making the transition away from being bicycles with engines. *Jeff Hackett*

Indian's wins were not limited to races in the United States. In 1911, Indian-mounted racers took first, second, and third at the Isle of Man—England's most famous race. That same year V. Davis set a new record for riding from New York to San Francisco: twenty days, nine hours, and eleven minutes, and that is with a complete engine overhaul on the way!

The following year, Charles B. Franklin rode 300 miles in under 300 minutes on a new 8-valve Indian. At the time, the mile-per-minute pace that he maintained was presumed to be as unbreakable a "barrier" as the sound barrier was to aircraft and pilots three decades later.

In 1914, Indian-mounted Cannonball Baker set a new west-to-east transcontinental record: eleven days, twelve hours, and ten minutes. Baker followed up that record with a "Three Flags" run from Canada to Mexico in a little over three days with a soon-to-be introduced Indian Powerplus. Two years later he set a new 1,000-mile record in twenty-one hours and three minutes in Australia.

Board-track racing, which goes back to at least 1908, was a popular event for fans around the country, although there was

The rider on this machine was called a "monkey-on-a-stick," and it is hard to imagine any racer finding this position comfortable. The downward-sloping seat forced the rider's rear backwards. When the rider grabbed the downswept grips and pegs, both his feet and hands were in front of his rear. *Jeff Hackett*

some question as to what they were coming to see. By the end of the race, the oval wooden tracks—some of which were former bicycle velodromes—were often slick with oil drippings from the bikes' total-loss oil systems.

There were many accidents and more than a few fatalities. That is not too surprising when you consider that helmets as we know them did not exist back then. Pictures from that era show that the racers often wore nothing on their heads, which may have looked good but provided next to no protection. Also, some racers reportedly were willing to do just about anything to win, including grabbing a competitor's handlebars.

If the potential for spills drew crowds, it also was to some degree responsible for the sport's demise. One particularly gruesome crash in New Jersey allegedly killed two racers and at least one young fan, who was struck by parts of one of the bikes. By the mid-1920s, board-track racing was on the decline, doomed to fade away.

Motorcycle racing, however, was by no means dying out—road racing and hillclimbing took over. Enter Ed Kretz, who won the first Daytona in 1937 with his Sport Scout, and then went on to win the first Laconia road races the next year.

In 1947 Max Bubeck amazed everyone by winning the prestigious Greenhorn Enduro on a modified Indian Four, a large and heavy machine not considered ideal for off-road racing. Bubeck later teamed up with

This engine may look small, but it is believed to be about 60 cubic inches and capable of putting out between 5 to 7 horsepower. It took a pedal-push jump start to get it going. This bike has not been started in years, but Greg Mazza, of Millwood Vintage Motorcycle Company in Millwood, New York, where the bike is kept, noted that it still has compression and he is convinced it could still run strong. "These motors don't know anything but to run. They'd work unless everything was falling apart," he said.
Jeff Hackett

Frank Chase to build a "Chout," basically a Chief engine shoehorned into a Scout 101 frame. The Chout's engine was modified to produce 65 horsepower at 4400 rpm. Capable of reaching speeds in excess of 135 miles per hour, it was the fastest non-streamlined Indian ever recorded.

Perhaps Indian's last racer was the short-lived Model 648 "Big Base" Daytona Sport Scout. Due to a changeover in Indian's management, only fifty or so of these machines were ever built for the 1948 lineup. One of

This year marked the end of the diamond-frame model, which is noteworthy for the rear cylinder being assembled as part of the frame itself. In 1909, the loop frame was introduced, and the rear cylinder was no longer part of the frame (although some leftover diamond-frame models were sold during 1909). The 1908 model was also very, very light. The civilian model weighed in at 120 pounds and came with a magneto. *Jeff Hackett.*

these machines won the Daytona races in both 1947 and 1948.

Before we say good-bye to the racing Indians, we must acknowledge Bert Munro and his 1920 side-valve Scout Bonneville racer. In 1926, his bike hit 54 miles per hour and he was hooked. He returned regularly and continued to increase his speeds. The machine was given an ever-growing displacement and eventually a streamliner body. In 1967, his forty-one-year-old Indian ran a one-way top speed of 190.07 miles per hour. This accomplishment makes the New Zealander's Scout the fastest Indian motorcycle of all time.

Riders not only had to beware of oily racing surfaces—some racers were not above yanking another competitor's handlebars. That may be why few parts—and no other 1908 Indian racer— are known to exist today. The racers came in either single- or twin-cylinder engines. The machines fared well—and so did Indian. That year, a total of 3,257 Indians were sold, and there were more than 400 Indian dealers across the country. *Jeff Hackett*

Bert Munro, a New Zealander who operated on a tight budget but with lots of ingenuity, converted a Scout engine into an overhead valve, 61-cubic-inch, fire-breathing monster. He modified just about every part of this engine, which features a four-cam setup. He is said to have taken a hacksaw, file, and even a rock or two to hammer out some of his modifications. *Gary Phelps*

Previous pages
Hard to believe, but underneath this sleek hull is a 1920 Model 596 Indian Scout. The legendary Bert Munro began work on this "Munro Special" in 1962. Over the next four to five years, he lengthened the wheelbase and made the streamlined outer shell to prepare it in his quest for speed records. *Gary Phelps*

The Munro Special scorched the Bonneville salt flats in 1967 with a speed of 190.07 miles per hour during its qualifying run. Munro set a class record with a two-way average of 183.586 miles per hour, more than 100 miles per hour faster than a stock 1920 Indian. *Gary Phelps*

Below
This shot helps you appreciate just how skillful and resourceful Munro was. He started with an old, old Indian, created a streamlined body, and made them go faster than any such combination had a right to do. He stopped racing the Munro Special after 1967, and it sat for years in storage, where time proved rather cruel to it. Steve Huntzinger and the late Dean Hensley restored the frame, fork, body, and exhaust to the condition you see here. *Gary Phelps*

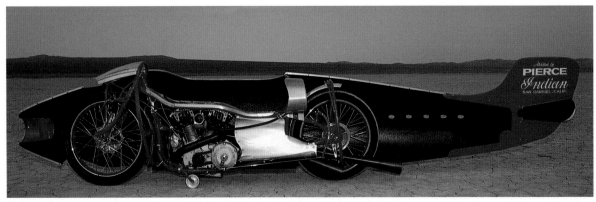

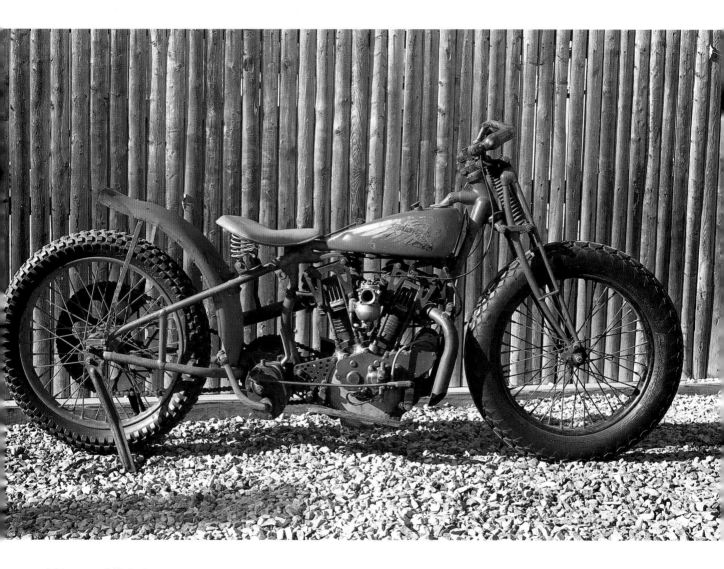

This 1924 hillclimber was campaigned for three decades (1934–1953) by racing great Howard Mitzell from York, Pennsylvania. It is a very rare model: the engine is one of twenty-five handmade in 1924 by Indian's experimental department. The 45-cubic-inch engine has overhead valves and developed 60 horsepower on alcohol. The bike is in original racing condition and has not been started in years, but it still has plenty of compression. *Jeff Hackett*

Look at that pipe and you can imagine how loud this Indian was when it roared up the hills. Howard Mitzell was a consistent winner on this machine, taking more than a hundred wins at hillclimb events. He was a "national first winner" several times. He raced the bike on the East Coast. Al Lauer campaigned it on the West Coast. *Jeff Hackett*

Right
Shown here with the bike are some of the trophies Howard Mitzell won over the years, his favorite yellow shirt, and his riding cap and helmet. It's also an example of how small the world can be. One month after collector Tony Penachio bought this bike in Los Angeles, California, he saw an ad on the East Coast for a box of memorabilia items for Howard Mitzell. He went to Springfield, Massachusetts, where he bought the box, which included the above listed items as well as more than 100 certificates of achievement for his wins. *Jeff Hackett*

You are looking at a pit box in front of the 1924 hillclimber. This is not the correct racing kit for this particular bike, but it was similar to what the Indian factory used. Inside this box are a variety of parts, including pistons, wristpins, cranks, transmission gears, primary chain drives, valves, pushrods, valve springs, exhaust intake, different cams, extra bearings, and hand tools. When a racing engine was built, a racing kit box was also prepared, and was marked with the same engine number. *Jeff Hackett*

1924

Indian

TWIN CYLINDER DAYTONA FRAME
SPEEDWAY RACER
WITH FLXI SIDECAR
EX-STEVE McQUEEN COLLECTION

Left
This 1924 twin-cylinder, Daytona-frame racer from the Steve McQueen collection features a Flxicar sidecar. To corner a sidecar back then, you had to muscle the handlebars through the turn. Not so with the Flxicar design. The Flxicar was mounted to the frame with two pivoting mounts. The sidecar's wheel was designed to remain parallel with the bike's wheels no matter what the angle the bike was leaned, which enabled the sidecar rig to go into a corner like a solo bike. How fast were they? In 1920, an Indian racing set a five-mile record time at a mile track with a time of 4:33:6. *Jeff Hackett*

The Flxicar sidecar rig was advertised as "the side car that tilts and turns but doesn't upset." Sidecars were the rage until a certain Henry Ford made it practical for the average person to own a car. This shot makes you wonder whether the designer ever planned to have the Flxicar double as a canoe. *Jeff Hackett*

This Indian speedway racer was originally built and raced by Noel McIntyre, who campaigned it successfully in southern California in the mid- to late 1920s and early 1930s. The speedway bike was nicknamed "The Harley Eater," and was a powerful machine built for experts. After McIntyre sold the bike, two racers who later owned it reportedly died riding it. The exact year of the bike is not known, although the modified frame is from a 1919-1927 Scout model. Harry Sucher, the noted Indian historian and author of *The Iron Redskin*, bought this racer without an engine, clutch assembly, or gearbox. With parts from his Powerplus collection and help from Dewey Bonkrud, they put in this 61-cubic-inch, "Big Valve" motor that uses pistons from an eight-cylinder Ford 302 engine. Combined with a Bosch magneto, port polishing, and slight cam profile changes, the engine is estimated to be capable of 34 horsepower at 4300 rpm.
Jeff Hackett

During a test run, Harry Sucher was able to ride this 285-pound bike at 70 miles per hour *at an idle*. In 1978, when the restoration was done, he took it up to the high 80s on a highway. He could have easily gone faster, but he was not anxious to push the racer, on its rickshaw clincher tires, to match the 100-plus miles per hour speed this racer used to zing along at in its heyday.
Jeff Hackett

Chapter 3

The Indian Scout

The Indian Scout was first conceived in the mind of Charles B. Franklin as Indian's midsize sport model and was introduced in 1919 for the 1920 model year. Originally powered by a 37-cubic-inch motor, it was increased to 45 cubic inches in 1927.

The early Scouts were fast and strong. In 1920, a Scout beat the existing twenty-four hour world's long distance record by covering an amazing 1,114 miles—250 miles more than the old record.

It was not until 1928 that the best handling Indian of all time was announced—the immortal Indian 101 Scout.

The 101 featured a combination of low seating and an extended wheelbase, which added up to nearly perfect handling. The handling is so impressive that the Indian 101 Scout is still much sought after and used by trick riders, including those who ride the Wall of Death, after almost seven decades of use.

The 101 Scout featured several innovations including an internal expanding front brake, a new magneto, a new carburetor, and a new oil pump. The 101 was also the first motorcycle to feature the continuous use of a unit construction powerplant (the larger Indian Chiefs did also).

Scouts were so well regarded as strong runners the factory slogan, "You can't wear out an Indian Scout," was expanded by Scout riders to say, "You can't wear out an

Opposite page
This is supposed to be a 1941 Sport Scout, but if it is, it was restored with personal taste in mind, not Antique Motorcycle Club of America judging. The un-Indian like mirrors no doubt were put on to make this a street legal bike, but the 1941 model did not have the Indian head painted on the gas tanks. The owner may have liked that touch so much that he just had it painted on anyway. The exhaust system also is not stock. *Jeff Hackett*

Indian Scout, or its brother the Indian Chief. They're built like rocks to take hard knocks; it's the Harleys that cause the grief."

The next major variation for the Scouts came in 1932 with the introduction of the Standard Scout. It was a much heavier machine than the 101 and it offered a longer wheelbase, allowing for the use of the larger chassis, transmission, and primary drive unit of the larger 74-cubic-inch Indian Chief. Abandoned in 1937, the Standard never reached the popularity of the 101 because most Scout riders never felt it was sporty enough.

In 1932 the Indian Scout Pony was introduced. It was their contribution to woo the entry-level rider into the Springfield family. It was lightweight in more than one sense. With only a 30.5-cubic-inch engine, it simply did not produce enough power to be exciting to the average Scout rider.

The following year, Indian tried another new Scout on their followers: the Moto-plane—which was basically a Pony with a

The fast, agile Scout adapted well to racing use, and many racers did just that. This 1928 101 Scout used as a hillclimber is an especially good example of a machine campaigned by a privateer. The racer was forced to retire because of injuries, but this machine was successfully raced as late as the 1960s. The frame was lengthened about two inches, and the front end is from a Prince, while the handlebars are from a mid-1930s model. It has both a kill switch on the bars and a separate shut-down system— a wire that was strapped around the rider's wrist and connected to the external points. *Jeff Hackett*

larger 45-cubic-inch engine. Unfortunately the Motoplane was another failure. The Motoplane's inexpensive and fragile transmission, clutch, and chassis borrowed from the Scout Pony simply could not withstand the extra power and literally destroyed themselves.

All was saved when the most famous Scout ever—the Sport Scout—was introduced in 1934. While close in size and dimensions to the unpopular Scout Pony, the Sport Scout was all new. It employed the tried and true keystone-type frame, mated with a unit-construction powerplant that used the Chief's rugged transmission gears.

The Sport Scout was far superior in performance and agility to every other motorcycle of that time, and it quickly became the machine to watch out for in all forms of motorcycle competition—hillclimbing, TT races, endurance races, and even Class C racing. It should be noted that Ed "Ironman" Kretz won the first Daytona motorcycle races and the first Laconia races on the same Indian Sport Scout.

Due to its popularity with the racers, a stock and original Sport Scout is now quite rare, as most were bought for competition and stripped down for the action. In spite of their being removed from Indian's product line in 1942, the Sport Scouts were still winning Class C races as late as 1956. In 1967 Indian dealer Bob Markey raced his side-valve flathead 1940 Sport Scout in the Open Class scrambles at the White Rose Motorcycle Club in York, Pennsylvania, (their last

Hillclimbers such as this one were frequently altered to reduce weight and improve handling. The side steering dampers are locked tight for stiff fork action. The two downtubes have been pulled in toward the motor, which pulls the neck of the bike down and helps keep the center of gravity low. There is little clearance between the magneto and the downtubes. The bike was also altered to accept a custom gas tank. The changes make the bike look as if it is leaning forward. *Jeff Hackett*

ever) and won, beating out an overhead-valve Harley-Davidson Sportster that was twenty-some years the Indian's junior.

Bob Markey still owns that racer as well as several others and keeps them in his shop, Bob's Indian Sales and Service in Etters, Pennsylvania.

Both the 101 and Sport Scouts performed miracles against the newer 1950s, 1960s, and even 1970s motorcycles in Class A hillclimbing. Perhaps one of the most amazing

Note the crudely broken cylinder fins. Owner Randy Zorn explained that the fins were deliberately broken off back then on competition bikes to reduce weight, which is especially a shame as these are hard-to-come-by square-faced Sport Scout cylinders. This 45 cubic-inch engine has been highly ported and polished. There is no oil pump; at that time the Scouts still operated on a total-loss system. The barrel-type, alcohol-burning Linkert carburetor was not set up for idling; it was either off or wide open. *Jeff Hackett*

victories went to the 45-cubic-inch Sport Scout that won the 1973 Class A National Championship Hillclimb held at the White Rose Motorcycle Club. The Scout outperformed all other machines—old and new!

The last machines to bear the Indian Scout name were the all-new 249 Scout motorcycles introduced in the summer of 1948 as a 1949 model. They were powered by a vertical-twin engine with overhead valves—very British in design and look. Many thought the modern look and style would have made it the best Scout ever, but it wasn't.

This new Scout was not created or developed by Indian's engineers. It was designed by a Connecticut firm named Torque. They sold the prototype and plans to the president of Indian Motocycles, Ralph B. Rodgers. Basically, the engine was a lightweight motor designed to be used in aircraft.

Indian was having serious financial problems and had plenty to deal with. In their rush to introduce the new Scout, there was little time to properly test the machine. The 249's reign of terror, unlike its predecessors, proved that almost everything that could go wrong with an all-new motorcycle would go wrong.

Due to the lack of acceptance of the new look and style, the 249 Scout did not sell well. Even the new ads portraying the 249 with movie stars, sports personalities, and race car drivers did little to boost their sales. It did not take long for problems to appear in the magnetos, generators, carburetors, and oil-circulation system. The construction was weak and the rear wheels were known to tear out the spokes at speed.

The Indian factory did what they could to correct these problems, but they were financially strapped. It is a shame because the machine had real possibilities. Perhaps too modern for its time, the 249 set a look and style for many motorcycles to follow.

After 249 production stopped in 1950, Indian never used the Scout name on another motorcycle. They did, however, use it on one of their bicycles.

Hillclimbers were built for one purpose only: to climb the steepest hills as fast as possible. Only high gear was used, the other transmission gears shaved away to save weight. If you wonder how a rider could take off in third gear, just take a look at the size of the rear sprocket, which is about four times the size of a stock unit. Even though top speed is just about 50 miles per hour, it took a lot of strength to control the "bucking bronco" ride. *Jeff Hackett*

Legend has it that a conversation in 1931 between the management of Indian and of the nearby Springfield Packard Car dealership led to the creation of the Dispatch-Tow. The three wheeler solved a nagging service problem. No longer would two people have to go to pick up a car and drive it back to the shop. Instead, one Dispatch-Tow mounted rider would go to the car, park in back, attach the yoke-type towing device fitted to the front axle to the car and drive away. When the car was done, he drove it back, unhitched the mount, and rode back. Nearly 400 were sold the first year. It was discontinued in 1932, but came back in 1935. *Courtesy of* Classic Cycle Review

Right
You don't see a lot of Dispatch-Tows today. Not only were they worked hard, the body was made of wood covered with tin, which you couldn't tell unless you looked underneath. Two size bodies were available: a standard one and a larger box with more carrying capacity. Of course, there was at least one more glamorous moment for the workhorse Dispatch-Tow: Cary Grant rode one with Irene Dunne in a chase scene in the movie *The Awful Truth. Courtesy of* Classic Cycle Review

This 1939 Dispatch-Tow was powered by a 45-cubic-inch engine. It was a Sport Scout from the seat post forward, with the exception of the towing device. But from the rear back it was a decidedly different animal. The low-compression engine, coupled with an automotive-style rear end, was well capable of towing cars. The Dispatch-Tow was not easy to handle at speeds of 50 miles per hour or over. *Courtesy of* Classic Cycle Review

The Sport Scout may look sporty from this rakish angle, but some Indian enthusiasts questioned whether it lived up to its name. The 1941 model weighed in at 500 pounds, 25 pounds more than the 1940 model and a full 115 pounds more than when it debuted in 1934. Many riders made it more fiery by stroking the 45-cubic-inch engine. Chopping the fenders was also a popular modification. *Jeff Hackett*

Left
The Indian company advertised the Sport Scout Dispatch-Tow as "The Only Means of Getting the Hurry-Up Job . . . The Cheapest Means of Getting Any Job." It touted the Indian for its fine features, noting: "The rear axle is of seamless tube construction. Differential is fully enclosed and of standard automotive type, having six bearings on the axle shafts. The chain drive operates a sprocket on the outside of differential housing—no chance for dust or dirt to enter." It also said the body leaf springs were controlled by "doublefriction snubbers," apparently a reference to the damping assembly. *Courtesy of* Classic Cycle Review

New for the 1941 Sport Scout was a spring frame for the former rigid. The exhaust "cuts" through the springs, which were mounted above and below the axles. The lower springs served as recoil dampers. The 1941 Scout also featured a new oil filter that the company claimed increased oil circulation by half. The external oil filter, which was not known for handling cold weather well (condensation on it froze) was eliminated. *Jeff Hackett*

The 1941 Sport Scout's rear shock system worked, but some Indian enthusiasts believe that it could have worked better. There wasn't a lot of difference in handling from the 1940 rigid model—both of which have a tendency to pogo about on rough roads. Elmer Lower observed that the system feels as if it was oversprung. *Jeff Hackett*

Left
This Fallon Brown and Indian Red 1941 Sport Scout is a 100-point restoration owned by Elmer Lower of Etters, Pennsylvania. It has the sixteen-inch wheels with painted rims, the first year they were offered as an option. The owner reports that there is not a major difference in handling than with the eighteen-inch tires. This bike needed work but was amazingly complete—the only missing parts were the generator belt cover and the horn back. *Jeff Hackett*

Previous pages
For a 1941 Sport Scout, it's easier to build the bike around the engine than to fit the motor into the frame. This engine is an integral part of the frame, not cradling it from below. It's easier to bolt the motor to the bottom plates, and attach the frame around it from there. The Chief's motor, however, sits on the frame as a non-supporting member, more easily removed. *Jeff Hackett*

The 1940-1941 Sport Scouts featured lighter pistons and newly styled cylinder barrels and heads. Indian claimed that the larger cooling fins significantly lowered oil temperature. The front fork rake was increased on the 1940-1941 Sport Scouts to improve the handling. In 1941, the solo seat also was made with an inch and a half of foam-rubber padding instead of the half-inch of horsehair. *Jeff Hackett*

This bike has a truly rare original piece of equipment: the battery. Lower said that he bought it in 1987 for $200, and had the interior fixed. The battery has the Indian script on the side. He said that it works better than the smaller batteries that he had previously used. The bike's high-output generator cooked two of them.
Jeff Hackett

M ost Indian shoppers overlook the Sport Scout in favor of the Chief. They don't know what they're missing!

—Jerry Hatfield,
Illustrated Indian Motorcycle
Buyer's Guide

Chapter 4

The Indian Chief

The Chief was the heavyweight of the Indian lineup. Even its name brings to mind images of supremacy, prestige, authority, and leadership. It was the American-made big twin that was, and to many still is, a symbol of this country's strength as a leader in manufacturing excellence, rarely equaled and never duplicated.

The brainchild of Charles B. Franklin, the Chief was first introduced late in 1921 for the 1922 sales season. Franklin was a naturally gifted student of motorcycle design with a strong background in race machinery. Hired by the Indian Motocycle Company in the mid-teens, he was the factory's first professionally trained engineer.

In very basic terms the Chief was a combination of the popular Powerplus, which had been introduced in 1916, and the dependable Scout, which had been first offered in 1920. Right off the showroom floor the Chief's solid, one-piece, Scout-style frame combined with its bullet-proof three-speed, integral gearbox and 42-degree, 61-cubic-inch V-twin engine produced a top speed of over 90 miles per hour, making a Chief *the* motorcycle to own. The Chief became a global sensation, destined to reign for over three decades.

Public and dealer demand for even more power brought Franklin back to the drafting board to create the 74-cubic-inch engine, which was introduced in 1923 as the "Big

Opposite page
This 1935 Chief won the award for best oldest restored Indian at Indian Day in 1992. Its owner, Ed Tortorico, Jr., of Port Chester, New York, rides it on a regular basis on the back roads. He reported that it's a strong runner although not without its foibles. Even though the seat post spring has lots of action, the Chief is relatively light (about 480 pounds), and the rigid rear end frame has a tendency to bounce about.
Buzz Kanter

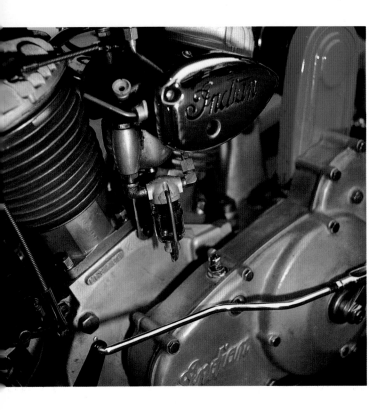

Ed Tortorico replaced the stock Schebler carburetor with a smoother running Linkert carburetor, but the 74-cubic-inch flathead engine is definitely capable of producing decent power when tweaked. A 1935 Chief ridden by Al Chasteen set a top speed of 125 miles per hour at Muroc Dry Lake in California in 1936. (Worth noting is that the top time of the day was set by a 1936 Indian Super Sport, ridden by Fred Lubow, who went 128.57 miles per hour.) *Buzz Kanter*

Chief." This style remained basically unchanged until 1927, when the fenders were restyled. The addition of a front brake in 1929 as well as the cast-aluminum fuel tanks in 1930 and 1931 completed the major changes in the first decade of the almighty Chief.

During the 1930s, the Chief helped Indian through one of the most economically disturbing, yet highly technical times this country has ever experienced. The Depression-era Chiefs, up until 1934, were produced in very limited quantities. People in the early 1930s were simply not buying much of anything, and a new motorcycle was never high on their lists. Indian struggled through those harsh times, constantly developing their motorcycles, and the Chiefs evolved and improved.

In 1932 the Chief was completely redesigned, sporting a new frame, front fork, eighteen-inch wheels with balloon tires, new electrics, restyled fuel tanks, and new fenders showed off the completely new engine design.

The first recirculating lubrication system use on an Indian motorcycle was introduced the following year—a major improvement over the total-loss oil system still being used on other brands.

In 1934 another innovative design was incorporated into the Chief: the addition of a primary chain, which replaced the rather dated helical-gear setup used to connect the transmission to the engine.

By 1935, the country was finally starting to come out of the Depression. Indian's production was stepped up a bit. The Chief's fenders enjoyed another restyling and the "Y" motor was introduced. It had improved breathing capability as well as heavier cylinders and larger head cooling fins for greater cooling efficiency and more horsepower.

One of the pluses of riding this three-speed Indian is that you always have a good feel for what gear you are in. The shift works directly off the transmission in what is called a "crotch shifter." If you wonder how it got that tag, look at the hand shifter and imagine trying to work through the gears. You could also get an optional four-speed, although it was not without its critics, who found it more difficult to shift and to find neutral. *Buzz Kanter*

The left side and the right rear side of the tank holds just gas while the right front section holds two quarts of oil for the total-loss oil system. Riders could expect to go through a half quart of oil in about 200 miles. *Buzz Kanter*

The leafspring front end, combined with the rigid frame, makes for a tough ride at certain speeds. But, there is a practical solution: either keep it under 50 miles per hour or above 60. As for the front brake, yes, it's there, but it was not much more than a complement to the rear brake that riders depended on. The front brake is nearly impossible to lock up. *Buzz Kanter*

This was also the first year the optional four-speed transmission was offered.

The fuel tanks were restyled once again in 1936 using the popular twist-on (bayonet) gas caps in place of the older threaded design. A new taillight and brakelight switch were also added.

The next year saw more changes: the rear fender was redesigned for a more "valanced" look to match the front fender, interchangeable front and rear wheels became the standard, and the oil pump was improved. The new pump worked so well that it was not changed for a decade.

The headlight and horn were interchanged in 1938 so that the Indian-faced horn was on top, creating a strong visual statement. A newly designed dash was used that year to allow the ignition switch, speedometer, and ammeter to be housed in an aluminum, heart-shaped dash atop the fuel tanks.

The powerful Bonneville model was added to the line in 1938. It allowed the rider extra power from the improved cams, lifters, cylinders, heads, carburetor, and magneto ignition.

The rigid-frame "open fender" Chief was last offered in 1939. They were the final models to be offered with the optional "World's Fair" paint design, making them one of the most attractive looking Chiefs of the decade.

The 1930s Chiefs, although not produced in large numbers, are quite popular with both collectors and restorers. Their rigid frames and open-style fenders gave

The country was finally escaping the doldrums of the Depression in 1935, and people were ready for a change. Indian gave the 1935 Chief a more graceful look through the use of new valanced fenders. The fenders were offered for two years only, and are hard to come by today. It's hard to see from this angle, but the rear taillight on this 1935 Chief comes from a 1936 model. In that year, the system incorporated the rear brake light. The owner has the correct part but had not changed it at the time these pictures were taken. *David Ruzga*

The changes for 1935 included a new chainguard, part of the overall move for more stylish look. Paint had long been an Indian specialty, and for 1935, customers could choose from three optional paint schemes and thirteen optional finishes. And for an extra $5, you could get any color made by the DuPont Company. *David Ruzga*

them a "looks fast even when standing still" style that never fails to attract attention wherever they are parked. Their low center of gravity, eighteen-inch wheels and leaf-spring front forks give them an easy handling feel that makes their ride an enjoyable and unforgettable experience.

As Indian moved into the 1940s, much of their attention was focused on the military effort. Even so, its newly redesigned civilian model Chief astounded the motorcycling world. Its full-skirted fenders and chain guard, new frame with sprung rear suspension, taller and smoother action front forks, and heavier-finned heads and cylinders created a look that is still being re-created today in modern production motorcycles.

Sixteen-inch wheels were introduced in 1941 giving the Chief a more gutsy look of distinction. The following year there were

no significant changes, and civilian models were rare. The 1943–1945 Chiefs were pretty much all bound for the military.

In 1946 the Chief emerged with a handsome new girder front fork—the first really major production design change in some twenty years. Sales volume also climbed significantly.

The only significant changes in the 1947 Chief were the addition of chrome—a commodity that had been in short supply during

The 1935 Chief featured a stock battery-and-coil ignition, although a magneto could be had as an option for $25. The change came about because starting it sometimes was tough, especially in colder climates. While a four-speed transmission was available for an extra $15, Indian also offered a transmission with three forward speeds and reverse. Those were used for several purposes, such as sidecar rigs and for commercial work setups. This was also the last year for the screw-in gas caps (in 1936, the bayonet-style caps were used). *David Ruzga*

When a rider topped 50 miles per hour, the vibration became more noticeable, but as V-twin riders still understand, the vibration made the ride seem that much more alive. The fork's trailing-link leafspring, almost invisible in this shot, staring straight at you (just below the horn), may not have been considered universally beautiful, but it did help the Indian steer true.
David Ruzga

the war years—and the introduction of the Indian-head fender light.

The 1948 Chief was graced with a new stamped-steel dash, housing a new speedometer with a larger diameter and a new face. The engine case was changed to house some internal improvements, and an aluminum oil pump was added. The speedometer drive was changed so that it was driven from the front wheel rather than from the rear wheel.

Because Indian was gearing up for the introduction of their British-made models, there was no Chief production in 1949.

During the 1950s, the handsome Indian Chief once again captured the public's imagination with their new and more powerful 80-cubic-inch powerplant complete with compensating sprocket to handle the increased torque between engine and transmission. The Chiefs were nearly identical in 1950 and 1951 with only minor cosmetic changes.

The 1952 and 1953 Chiefs were the last of the proud line. They sported re-styled fenders, fuel tanks, exhaust systems, seats, and a host of other smaller details in a last ditch effort to save a company well past its prime.

These last Chiefs are some of the most sought after collectible motorcycles in the world today. They can be obtained and restored, and, with a minimum of maintenance, can be used as daily transportation while still retaining their full appraised value. How many other motorcycles can you say that about?

This 1936 Indian Chief was built out of parts in late 1987 and 1988 by owner Elmer Lower of Etters, Pennsylvania. It has received its junior and senior first standing, getting a 100-point score from the Antique Motorcycle Club of America. Lower started with a frame and cases that had matching numbers, and pieced the rest together with help from Bob and Robin Markey, of Bob's Indian, and by scouring the tables at flea markets. The hardest part to find? This was the last year for the non pre-focused headlight assembly. The 1936 model features an adjustment screw that moved the bulb in and out to diffuse the light. Elmer Lower reports that it is a nice touch, but is not especially good for night riding. *Jeff Hackett*

Left

1936 was the last year for this shifter, which ran directly off the transmission. Elmer Lower said that it is so easy to shift he can do it with his knee. He has put nearly 11,000 miles on since he restored it, and enjoys riding it with his wife Jo. "The bikes were made to be ridden, so that's what I do," he said. *Jeff Hackett*

What makes a 100-point Indian? This 1936 Chief only has chrome that was offered in the original Indian accessory package. Judges do not necessarily favor additional chrome, even if it was available. No part should ever be powder-coated. Also, If new hardware is being used, any stamps or markings should be ground off, and the part glass beaded so it doesn't shine. And stainless-steel spokes are okay, but glass bead them as well. The saddlebags are reproductions made from an original set Lower once owned. *Jeff Hackett*

This 1947 Chief, owned by Gary Stark and painted by his father, Bob, features a rare Rainbow paint job. Gary's grandfather, Charles, was one of the first Indian dealers in the country. John Polivik, an employee at the Akron, Ohio, shop in the 1940s, created the tricky Rainbow paint scheme, which the Indian factory tried but could not duplicate in quality. So, when an order came in for a Rainbow, Indian shipped the tin to the shop, where John gave it his magic touch and then sent it back. By the way, a two-tone red with yellow trim was the most popular combination. *Roy Kidney*

Right
This close-up gives you an idea just how demanding it was to create a Rainbow paint job. Bob Stark, who has done more than thirty himself, said that the taping element alone makes this multi-level paint job extremely labor intensive. He noted that it was much more difficult back in the 1940s to do this work because the painters didn't have the same painting equipment as is available today; they needed an ultra-fine touch. *Roy Kidney*

A devoted Indian lover may feel that the color of this 1947 Indian Chief is wrong, but there are two schools of thought on that. For $5 extra, Indian would paint your bike any color made by DuPont. This color, Kashun Green, was only offered in 1940, but the owner of this Indian liked the shade so much that he decided he just had to have it. Whatever, it is such a thorough restoration that color notwithstanding, the judges have awarded it a senior first show. *Dave Ruzga*

Right
The 1947 Chief is quite similar to the 1946 model, with most of the changes of a cosmetic nature. Top speed for the 1946 and 1947 Chiefs was said to be 85 miles per hour, upped to 95 with polished ports and precision ignition timing. The Bonneville model, which had major top-end work, including special cams, could top 100 miles per hour. Not bad, considering that the Chief was a flathead and weighed in at 550 pounds. *Dave Ruzga*

T he skirted-fender era began in 1940, with all the Indian models getting the streamline treatment. Riders either loved or hated the new fenders; there was no in-between.

—Jerry Hatfield,
Illustrated Indian Motorcycle Buyer's Guide

The distinctive Indian head emblem was gone in 1947, replaced by the script lettering you see here. This was the last year for the one-piece exhaust system that had been first used the previous year. Starting with the 1948 model, a clamp by the kickstarter connected the one-piece front and rear-exhaust headers to the muffler and tailpipe assembly. *Dave Ruzga*

One major change made in the 1946–1947 model years was the use of the girder fork front end. The approximately three extra inches of front axle travel made for a smoother ride than the prior leafspring units. More chrome was also available on the 1947 models, which was due to the end of the war and the more ready supply of precious metals that had previously been reserved for the war effort. *Dave Ruzga*

The 74-cubic-inch Chief engine was known for torque more than for horsepower. Its flathead design was not as modern as the overhead-valve design used in the contemporary Harley-Davidson knuckleheads, but the Indian engine was simpler and more reliable than the Harley-Davidson engine. *Gary Phelps*

S kirted-fender Chiefs turn heads among any group of motorcyclists. During the 30,000 miles I put on my 1947 Chief, every time I rode the bike at least one person gave me a thumbs-up or a grin.

—Jerry Hatfield,
*Illustrated Indian Motorcycle
Buyer's Guide*

The 1948 Indian Chief had the first instrument panel revamp since ten years earlier. The new speedometer, which featured a Stuart-Warner speedometer with a needle shaped like an arrow, was driven from the front wheel. *Gary Phelps*

The 1948 Chief was the last model to use the 74-cubic-inch engine that Indian had been using since 1923. It was replaced in 1950 (few 1949 Indian Chiefs were built because the factory was moving) by the 80-cubic-inch engine. The 1948 model Chief also featured the last girder front end, which was replaced by the telescopic system. *Gary Phelps*

Both the police and civilian models were strong runners, capable of topping 100 miles per hour. Indian returned to a rear wheel drive speedometer setup that had been discontinued in 1947. The buddy seat, which is original to 1952 and 1953 and unusual in that it does not rest on the seat post, is an especially hard item to track down. This Indian is owned by Randy Zorn. *David Ruzga*

Following pages
You can expect to pay top dollar for an Indian made in 1953, the final year of true Indian production motorcycles, While the 1952 and 1953 models were quite similar, this 1953 Roadmaster is especially rare because it was one of a handful of civilian models made (they used Amal carbs vs. the Linkert for the police models). One change was the addition of the engine cowling, which hid the oil pump and distributor. Another was the raising of the foot clutch lever about an inch to increase foot leverage so the clutch brake assembly could be activated easier. *David Ruzga*

Chapter 5

The Indian Four—
Two Wheeled Luxury

In the first quarter century of motorcycling in America, there were several manufacturers of four-cylinder motorcycles—Ace, Cleveland, Henderson, and Pierce.

The Henderson brothers, Will and Tom, sold their business to bicycle magnate Ignatz Schwinn. They worked for him for a while before setting out on their own in 1920 to build the Ace four-cylinder motorcycle.

In 1927 Indian purchased the Ace company and franchised Indian dealers were the first to offer a complete line of motorcycles when they added the 395-pound Indian Ace Four to their line of single and twin-cylinder motorcycles.

The man who designed the Ace motorcycle, W. G. Henderson, was the champion of the four-cylinder-motorcycle concept. He first manufactured his successful four-cylinder machines in 1912 and continued to improve his basic designs until his death in

1922. The Ace was without question his most refined design, one that lived on as the basis for Indian's four-cylinder machines.

By 1927 the "new" Indian Four was the talk of the town. It appeared in glorious color on the cover of *Indian News*, the manufacturer's own publication.

Indian's literature in 1929 emphasized the heavier machine's smoothness and ample power. Before becoming an Indian factory engineer, Art Lemon worked with Hender-

Opposite page
In 1937, two Zenith carburetors replaced the single Marvel updraft carburetor used the previous year. The Zenith carburetors were more finicky than the single Marvel, but they produced more horsepower. The carburetors, by the way, were individually jetted; the front was jetted number 14 (drill size) while the rear was number 17. Why? The rear cylinder heated up more, so the richer mixture helped keep it cooler.
Jeff Hackett

The Super Four's motor is connected to the frame by four bolts. The ride is relatively smooth, but as for the brakes . . . well, Indian riders don't brag about them for a reason. Unless it was a perfectly matched setup, the front brake was not much good. It also was no simple task for a lone rider to put this Indian on the rearstand. *Jeff Hackett*

son on developing the Four. While in the Springfield factory, Lemon further improved the basic engine by adding a five-main-bearing design as well as a stronger crankshaft in 1929.

Left
This 1937 Sport Four, a former police bike meticulously restored by Rudy Litke, shows just how good a fine touch the Indian factory offered when it came to finishes. For a few dollars more, riders could get any special colors available in DuPont Deluxe. Riders could also get pencil stripe (very fine) or pen stripe (thicker) detailing. *Jeff Hackett*

After five years of production, the Indian Four was renamed the Model 403 in 1932. It was given a larger and stronger frame, streamlined saddle tanks, heavier forks, and new fenders. Unfortunately the weight continued to climb; the Four now weighed in at 500 pounds.

Many of the changes were implemented as part of a plan to standardize parts and cut costs wherever possible. The same wheels, brakes, forks, fenders, tanks, saddles, and other various hardware were used on all models. While some individuals might have seen this move as removing some of the per-

For the 1937 model year, the hand shift was moved about a half foot forward. This was a case of good news, bad news: the good news was that the rider's knee no longer banged into it. The bad news was that it was much easier to miss a shift because the longer linkage to the shift tower on the transmission resulted in slop. *Jeff Hackett*

sonality of each machine, because it worked, it did produce one very handsome line of motorcycles. These designs were used throughout the early 1930s.

The big news for the Indian Fours in 1935 was the new, handsome, streamlined fenders and the large variety of color options available directly from the factory.

The Indian Four was never an inexpensive machine. It carried a high price tag and too many enthusiasts coming out of the Depression found it was simply too expensive, so the four-cylinder model did not sell in large numbers. The Indian Four was a handsome, comfortable, and fast machine, but it was not affordable to most.

The unpopular "upside-down" motor replaced the more traditional design in 1936, some twenty-four years after the basic design was first made available to the motorcycling public.

It was called "upside-down" because the engineers had reversed the valve arrangement by placing the exhaust valves on top of the engine and the intake valves on the side. To those accustomed to the older design this new design looked a bit odd. It achieved a significant power increase, but did nothing for their sales.

The short-lived upside-down Four was available only in 1936, and 1937 it was never much of a success.

Always looking for better sales, Indian redesigned the Four again in 1938, creating perhaps the most beautiful Indian Four ever produced. The new engine design boasted handsome cylinders cast in pairs, with clean, wider fins. The machine was also equipped with new tappets and rockers that were encased in aluminum finned covers, as well as handsome new instrument panels and new paint offerings.

The road systems were improving by 1938, and the pace of traffic was on the rise. The Indian Four needed greater speed and power for the longer distances. Fortunately, these machines could glide along at 5 miles per hour or rocket out at 100 miles per hour without a complaint.

Full-valanced fenders and spring-and-

Except for some minor cosmetic changes, the 1939 Indian Four is identical to the 1938 model, which represented a drastic and welcome change from the ill-fated "upside-down" 1936 and 1937 Four. The upside-down tag came from the reversal of the valve configuration. Not only that, the 1936 and 1937 Fours didn't win too many fans over when their exhaust system displayed a disturbing tendency to burn a rider's leg. *Jeff Hackett*

James Anderson of Melrose Park, Illinois, owns this 1939 blue and silver Four. The 1938 and 1939 Fours represented sweeping changes from the 1937 model in many ways. The 77-cubic-inch engine featured major advancements: larger cooling fins, a better manifold, cylinders cast in pairs, and all the tappet and rocker gears were enclosed and better lubricated. *Jeff Hackett*

plunger rear frames were introduced in 1940. The weight had climbed once again, this time to 568 pounds, up seventy-three pounds from the original Indian Ace.

In 1941, the only significant change was the addition of the larger sixteen -inch tires to improve the machines road-handling ability, as well as improve the motorcycle's appearance.

Nineteen forty-two saw the United States heavily involved in World War II. Few civilian Indians were produced. The Four was not seen as appropriate for military use, so its production was halted. After the war ended, the Indian management choose to focus on the lighter, less expensive, twin-cylinder models.

The Indian Four was the last of the long line of American four-cylinder motorcycles. It should be noted that Max Bubeck successfully raced an Indian Four well into the late 1940s, and managed to win the 1947 Greenhorn Enduro with his "old and obsolete" Indian Four.

It should also be noted that two experimental Indian Fours were hand built during the war years. The larger of the two was a 61-cubic-inch overhead-valve model built in 1941. It had a hand clutch, foot shift, and a driveshaft and was often being ridden on the streets around the factory.

The second experimental Indian Four (the Torque Four) was purchased by Indian when in 1945 they bought out a motorcycle company called the Torque Manufacturing Company in nearby Plainville, Connecticut. It had been founded by the Stockvis brothers from Belgium.

Indian management moved this project into the Springfield facilities and turned it over to G. Briggs Weaver. The engine displaced 54 cubic inches. It also featured a driveshaft and a four-speed transmission with foot shift and hand clutch. This was a small, light, and effective machine.

Unfortunately, neither of these two experimental Fours were ever seriously considered for production because neither were properly developed and both were costly designs to manufacture. Because Indian was not interested in low production numbers or expensive machines, they focused all their attention elsewhere, ending the saga of the Indian Four.

When it came to appearance, the 1938 and 1939 Indian Four's new sweeping mudguards, switch receptacle, and aluminum instrument nacelle convinced some Indian buffs that these were the best looking Indians to date. Still, owners of the Fours continued to have problems with its single-plate clutch, especially when it was cold or if the bike had been sitting long. A cure was not forthcoming until 1965, when a pressure plate with Neoprene inserts was invented. *Jeff Hackett*

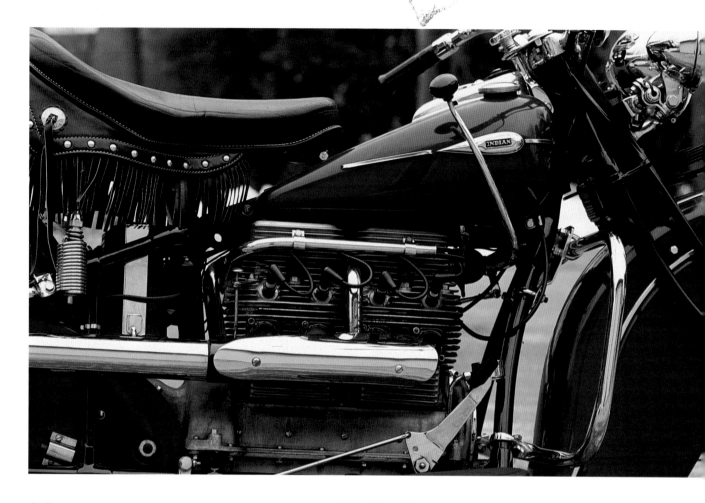

Left
The 1939 Indian Four weighed thirty-six pounds less than the 1940 model, which was a hefty 568 pounds. While this restoration is generally top-notch, the stock 1939 model came with a screwed-in air cleaner. *Jeff Hackett.*

This 1941 Four is a national points winner owned by Rudy Litke. If you look to the left of the first spark plug, you will see a small choke-like device that often is missing on restored Indians. It was used for cold weather riding. The rider pulled the choke, which closed a butterfly in the exhaust manifold. That, in turn, diverted hot gases to the front exhaust through heat-riser tubes that plugged into the manifold. Over the years, some of the chokes were removed while others fell victim to corrosion. *Jeff Hackett*

This is the ultimate old motorcycle for touring. With an oil cooler and modified oil passages, a late Four like this can cruise all day at 70. Out on the road, for a twelve-hour day, this motorcycle can't be touched by anything else older than a Gold Wing.

—Jerry Hatfield,
Illustrated Indian Motorcycle
Buyer's Guide

The Four's stock 77-cubic-inch engine was capable of taking the Indian over 90 miles per hour—over 100 with a few changes—yet it could slow to a walking pace in high gear. The 1941 model was nearly identical to the 1940 model with the exception of minor chrome trim changes. This Indian Four has been well restored. But, if you look at the rear of the seat, you will see a . . . gasp! . . . small Harley bracket under the buddy seat. Why? Ask Rudy.
Jeff Hackett

Left

The leafspring front end was adjustable for rider weight. The main headlight and two-spotlight setup may look good, but in reality few riders ever rode far with all the lights turned on. The subsequent drain was just too much for the generator, so riders would use the main beam alone. This was also the first year for sealed headlights, which proved to be superior to the bulb-type lights used on previous Fours. *Jeff Hackett*

The Indian and the Harley factories may have their disagreements in philosophy, but there was one area they both agreed: when it came time for advertising their motorcycles, this was *not* the side of the bike they would show. The Fours (and Harleys) look much better on the exhaust side. *Jeff Hackett*

This Indian Four prototype belongs to Dr. John "Doc" Patt of Pennsylvania, a long-time judge with the Antique Motorcycle Club of America. This Model 49 Torque Four was hand built by Indian in 1948–1949, but never went into production. If it had, Doc predicted it would have had tough going because of several design flaws. *Jeff Hackett*

Doc reported that this Four's kickstarter was not very good. Each kick would only rotate the engine about a quarter of a turn. Turning it over on a cold morning would not have been easy.

The flywheel was also too light for the combined weight of the four pistons and crankshaft, so inertia was far from ideal. *Jeff Hackett*

C ruising around the parking lot of an antique motorcycle meet, at idle or putting along, this baby makes motorcycling's king of sounds.

—Jerry Hatfield,
Illustrated Indian Motorcycle Buyer's Guide

The headlight and taillight you see mounted on the bike are there just for looks. When he took the engine apart, Doc found that provisions had been made for fitting a generator drive off the rear of the camshaft, but the designers didn't fit a drive gear into the cavity they'd cast on the crankcase. Note the location of those high exhaust pipes! *Jeff Hackett*

The Four is the greatest motorcycle showpiece, the Duesenberg of motorcycling.

—Jerry Hatfield,
Illustrated Indian Motorcycle Buyer's Guide

Doc, who likes to work on his machines, needed a local machine shop to replace a handmade helical-cut spur gear that had cracked, and was responsible for making an odd noise in the transmission. He couldn't machine the precise geometric curves on each tooth, so he found a machine shop that was able to do it using the old one as a pattern. *Jeff Hackett*

When the engine was right, Doc tried several carburetors before settling on a Schebler. He noted that before he got and restored this Four, someone had to have ridden it because there was carbon in the exhaust pipe. How's it run? Doc admitted that it doesn't idle well and it is difficult to start, which is due to the light flywheel and possibly to the intake manifold, which was also not well designed. But, "at speed it's delightful to drive and it handles well." *Jeff Hackett*

Indian-Related Motorcycle Clubs and Magazines

Clubs

All-American Indian Motorcycle Club
25801 Clark Rd.
Wellington, OH 44090
$10 a year (four newsletters per year).

Antique Motorcycle Club of America
Box 333
Sweetzer, IN 46987
$20 per year (four magazine per year).

Indian Four Cylinder Club
Rt. 2, Box 227
Rosedale, IN 47874
$15 per year (four newsletters per year).

Indian Motorcycle Club of America
Box 1743
Perris, CA 92370
$25 per year (twelve newsletters per year).

Indian Motorcycle News
Box 455
Lake Elsinore, CA 92330

Laughing Indian Riders
1114 237A St. RR 9
Langley, BC V3A 6H5 Canada
$12 per year (four newsletters per year).

101 Association
679 Riverside Ave.
Torrington, CT 06790
$15 per year (four booklets per year).

Magazines

American Iron Magazine
P.O. Box 506
Mt. Morris, IL 61054
(815) 734-1101
By far America's best Harley and Indian magazine. Plenty of great color photos and no scantily clad women, obscene language, or outlaw attitudes. $25 per year (twelve issues).

Bike Journal International
P.O. Box 391
Mt. Morris, IL 61054
(815) 734-1101
The best-selling vintage and classic bike magazine in America. A great combination of articles, tech pieces, and some of the best classifieds anywhere. A good place to buy or sell Indians and parts. $24.95 per year (twelve issues).

Classic Cycle Review
641-645 Seneca St.
Harrisburg, PA 17110
A handsome magazine featuring older motorcycles of all makes. Plenty to read and nice photos. $24 per year (six issues).

Indian Motorcycle Illustrated
6 Prowitt St.
Norwalk, CT 06855
(203) 855-0008
A new, high-class publication dedicated to Indian motorcycles. Plenty of Indians featured in full color, along with technical and history pieces.

Indian Motorcycle News
Box 455
Lake Elsinore, CA 92330
Great reprints of older Indian articles, technical, and restoration information. $25 per year (six issues).

Index